Reflections on a Gift of
WATERMELON PICKLE...

AND OTHER MODERN VERSE

POINTS *of* DEPARTURE

Reflections on a Gift of
WATeRMeLON PiCKlE...

AND OTHER MODERN VERSE
SECOND EDITION

COMPILED BY

STEPHEN DUNNING

EDWARD LUEDERS

NAOMI SHIHAB NYE

KEITH GILYARD

DEMETRICE A. WORLEY

ScottForesman
A Division of HarperCollins*Publishers*

EDITORIAL OFFICES: Glenview, Illinois
REGIONAL OFFICES: Sunnyvale, California • Tucker, Georgia
• Glenview, Illinois • Oakland, New Jersey • Dallas, Texas

AUTHORS

STEPHEN DUNNING, author, editor, and educator, writes poetry and fiction that has been widely published in magazines and anthologies. Retired from the University of Michigan, Dunning, a former president of the National Council of Teachers of English, has published several titles for teaching poetry in the classroom and has consulted in forty-nine states. He, along with Edward Lueders and the late Hugh Smith, compiled the first editions of *Reflections on a Gift of Watermelon Pickle* and *Some Haystacks Don't Even Have Any Needle.* His awards include five PEN Syndicated Fiction Awards, Creative Artist grants from the Michigan Council for the Arts, and the James B. Hall Fiction Award from Jazz Press.

EDWARD LUEDERS is a teacher, writer, and editor who serves as a member of the writing faculty at Breadloaf School of English, Middlebury College, Vermont. Retired from the University of Utah, where he served as English Department Chair and Director of Creative Writing, Lueders has consulted with students as a Poet-in-the-Schools for thirty years. He collaborated with Stephen Dunning and the late Hugh Smith on *Reflections on a Gift of Watermelon Pickle* and *Some Haystacks Don't Even Have Any Needle* and with Primus St. John on *Zero Makes Me Hungry.* His honors include a fellowship in creative writing from the National Endowment for the Arts and the Utah Governor's Award in the Humanities.

NAOMI SHIHAB NYE has worked as a visiting Writer-in-the-Schools at all grade levels for twenty years. She has conducted poetry workshops across the country and worked as a visiting poet/lecturer in the Middle East and Asia for the Arts America program of the U.S. Information Service. Her honors include: winner of the National Poetry Series, the Charity Randall Prize for Spoken Poetry from the International Poetry Forum, the I.B. Lavan Award for Younger Poets from the Academy of American Poets, and three Pushcart Prizes. Her anthology of poems for younger readers, *This Same Sky,* was named a Notable Book by the American Library Association.

KEITH GILYARD, Professor of Writing and English at Syracuse University, spent fourteen years as a professor at City University of New York teaching courses in creative writing, African American literature, composition, and poetry. He received his M.F.A. from Columbia's Writing Program and his doctorate in English Education from NYU. He has published a collection of poetry, *American Forty,* and a memoir, *Voices of the Self,* for which he won an American Book Award in 1992.

DEMETRICE A. WORLEY is an Assistant Professor of English and Coordinator of Writing at Bradley University in Peoria, Illinois, where she teaches creative writing, African American literature, composition, and technical writing. Her poetry has appeared in such literary journals as *Rambunctious Review, Poet,* and *The Spoon River Quarterly.* She is the co-author with Jesse Perry, Jr. of *African American Literature: An Anthology of Nonfiction, Fiction, Poetry, and Drama.*

ISBN: 0–673–29423–4
Acknowledgments for quoted matter and illustrations are included in the acknowledgments section on pages 170–177. The acknowledgments section is an extension of the copyright page.

789-DQ-0403020100

CONTENTS

NOTE

Almost thirty years have passed since the first poems were selected for *Reflections on a Gift of Watermelon Pickle . . . and Other Modern Verse.* Those poems have delighted students, teachers, and parents of several generations. This second edition keeps the best of the best, poems that teachers singled out as their students' favorites, and adds eighty new poems to the mix. Here are four ideas that will help you read the poems in this new collection:

1. Take your time in judging each poem. Poems don't spring from poets' brains. Poets spend more hours finding right words than you will spend minutes reading them. If a word or a line confuses you at first, try to discover why the poet may have left it just as he did.

2. Read each poem slowly. Give every poem a chance to speak to you. Reread. Read aloud. Make your ears and your eyes work on each poem. Expect to find surprises—then read slowly enough to enjoy them.

3. Read only a few poems at one time. The language of poetry is condensed. You will have to supply words that are missing and puzzle over lines that aren't clear at first reading. Better to read one or two poems well than to read a dozen poems carelessly.

4. Judge poems by their quality, not by their subjects. You may not like cats, but there are good cat poems. You may not like (or even believe in) flying saucers, but whether you do or don't has no bearing on the quality of "Southbound on the Freeway" (page 86). You may like love poems or hate love poems, but that has nothing to do with how well or how badly young love is described in "Adolescence—I" (page 35). Read each poem with the idea that you will "let" the poet write on any subject he chooses and in any way he chooses.

Perhaps the best advice of all is in the following poem:

How to Eat a Poem

by Eve Merriam

Don't be polite.
Bite in.
Pick it up with your fingers and lick the juice that
*   may run down your chin.*
It is ready and ripe now, whenever you are.

You do not need a knife or fork or spoon
or plate or napkin or tablecloth.

For there is no core
or stem
or rind
or pit
or seed
or skin
to throw away.

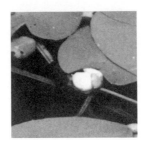

Unfolding Bud

One is amazed
By a water-lily bud
Unfolding
With each passing day,
Taking on a richer color
And new dimensions.

One is not amazed,
At a first glance,
By a poem,
Which is as tight-closed
As a tiny bud.

Yet one is surprised
To see the poem
Gradually unfolding,
Revealing its rich inner self,
As one reads it
Again
And over again.

Naoshi Koriyama

Gone Forever

Halfway through shaving, it came—
the word for a poem.
I should have scribbled it
on the mirror with a soapy finger,
or shouted it to my wife in the kitchen,
or muttered it to myself till it ran
in my head like a tune.

But now it's gone with the whiskers
down the drain. Gone forever,
like the girls I never kissed,
and the places I never visited—
the lost lives I never lived.

Barriss Mills

For Poets

by Al Young

Stay beautiful
but don't stay down underground too long
Don't turn into a mole
or a worm
or a root
or a stone

Come on out into the sunlight
Breathe in trees
Knock out mountains
Commune with snakes
& be the very hero of birds

Don't forget to poke your head up
& blink
Think
Walk all around
Swim upstream

Don't forget to fly

Talking Drums # 1

by Khephra

Carved from that same tree
in another age
counsel/warriors who
in the mother tongue
made drums talk
now in another tongue
make words to walk in rhythm
'cross the printed page
carved from that same tree
in another age

To Look

at

Any Thing

To look at any thing,
If you would know that thing,
You must look at it long:
To look at this green and say
'I have seen spring in these
Woods,' will not do—you must
Be the thing you see:
You must be the dark snakes of
Stems and ferny plumes of leaves,
You must enter in
To the small silences between
The leaves,
You must take your time
And touch the very peace
They issue from.

John Moffitt

Good Hotdogs

For Kiki

Fifty cents apiece
To eat our lunch
We'd run
Straight from school
Instead of home
Two blocks
Then the store
That smelled like steam
You ordered
Because you had the money
Two hotdogs and two pops for here
Everything on the hotdogs
Except pickle lily
Dash those hotdogs
Into buns and splash on
All that good stuff
Yellow mustard and onions
And french fries piled on top all
Rolled up in a piece of wax
Paper for us to hold hot
In our hands
Quarters on the counter
Sit down
Good hotdogs
We'd eat
Fast till there was nothing left
But salt and poppy seeds even
The little burnt tips
Of french fries
We'd eat
You humming
And me swinging my legs

Sandra Cisneros

Blueberry Pie

It was blueberry pie
and the crust was rolled
and folded and flaked and baked
and the heat of the summer day
blended with the heat of the oven
and grandma as pink as a sunset
kissed my cheek with her soft wet
cheeks and the pie splattered blue ooze
on the oven floor and there was only
blueberry air and she peeked in the oven
and it was cooking and grandma said "good"
"it will be ready soon" and she took a spoon
in one hand and me in the other and we opened
the oven door once more and the hot winds slapped
my face and grandma scraped the viscous blue and handed
me the spoon and the burning blue kissed my lips
and we smiled blue all day.

Nancy Gorrell

August

When the blackberries hang
swollen in the woods, in the brambles
nobody owns, I spend

all day among the high
branches, reaching
my ripped arms, thinking

of nothing, cramming
the black honey of summer
into my mouth; all day my body

accepts what it is. In the dark
creeks that run by there is
this thick paw of my life darting among

the black bells, the leaves; there is
this happy tongue.

Mary Oliver

Knoxville, Tennessee

I always like summer
best
you can eat fresh corn
from daddy's garden
and okra
and greens
and cabbage
and lots of
barbecue
and buttermilk
and homemade ice-cream
at the church picnic
and listen to
gospel music
outside
at the church
homecoming
and go to the mountains with
your grandmother
and go barefooted
and be warm
all the time
not only when you go to bed
and sleep

Nikki Giovanni

Eating Together

In the steamer is the trout
seasoned with slivers of ginger,
two sprigs of green onion, and sesame oil.
We shall eat it with rice for lunch,
brothers, sister, my mother who will
taste the sweetest meat of the head,
holding it between her fingers
deftly, the way my father did
weeks ago. Then he lay down
to sleep like a snow-covered road
winding through pines older than him,
without any travelers, and lonely for no one.

Li-Young Lee

Comida

by Victor M. Valle   **Food**

Uno se come   *One eats*
la luna en la tortilla   *the moon in a tortilla*
Comes frijol   *Eat frijoles*
y comes tierra   *and you eat the earth*
Comes chile   *Eat chile*
y comes sol y fuego   *and you eat sun and fire*
Bebes agua   *Drink water*
y bebes cielo   *and you drink sky*

Salad

The woman
did not mean to
offend me,

her blue eyes
blinking
at the glint
of my blade,

as I cut
precisely
like magic
the cucumber in
exact, even,
quick slices.

Do you orientals
do everything
so neatly?

Janice Mirikitani

Absolutes

(From an ink painting by Seiho)

black on white
crow in snow
          hunched
          wet lump
on brittle branch
remembering warmth
remembering corn
miserable
as life
is
black on white

Gustave Keyser

Crows

I like to walk
And hear the black crows talk.

I like to lie
and watch crows sail the sky.

I like the crow
That wants the wind to blow:

I like the one
That thinks the wind is fun.

I like to see
Crows spilling from a tree,

And try to find
The top crow left behind.

I like to hear
Crows caw that spring is near.

I like the great
Wild clamor of crow hate

Three farms away
When owls are out by day.

I like the slow
Tired homeward-flying crow;

I like the sight
Of crows for my good night.

David McCord

A Trip on the Staten Island Ferry

Dear Jonno
there are pigeons who nest
on the Staten Island Ferry
and raise their young
between the moving decks
and never touch
ashore.

Every voyage is a journey.

Cherish this city
left you by default
include it in your daydreams
there are still   secrets
in the streets
even I have not discovered
who knows if the old men
shining shoes on the Staten Island Ferry
carry their world   in that box
slung across their shoulders
if they share their lunch
with the birds flying
back and forth
on an endless journey
if they ever find their way
back home.

Audre Lorde

Wild Goose

He climbs the wind above
  green clouds of pine,
Honking to hail the
  gathering migration,
And, arching toward the
  south, pulls to align
His flight into the great
  spearhead formation.

He'll find a bayou land of
  hidden pools,
And bask amid lush fern
  and water lily
Far from the frozen world
  of earth-bound fools
Who, shivering, maintain
  that geese are silly.

Curtis Heath

Some Brown Sparrows

Some brown sparrows who live
in the Bronx Zoo visit often
the captive Victoria Crested
Pheasant, visit captive Peacocks,
Cockatoos. They fly through bars
to visit also monkeys, jackals,
bears. They delouse themselves in
cage dust, shaking joyously;
they hunt for bread crumbs, seeds
or other tidbits. Briefly,
they lead free sparrow lives
and fly free.

Bruce Fearing

Seal

See how he dives
  From the rocks with a zoom!
   See how he darts
    Through his watery room
     Past crabs and eels
     And green seaweed,
     Past fluffs of sandy
     Minnow feed!
     See how he swims
      With a swerve and a twist,
     A flip of the flipper,
     A flick of the wrist!
     Quicksilver-quick,
    Softer than spray,
   Down he plunges
  And sweeps away;
 Before you can think,
Before you can utter
Words like "Dill pickle"
Or "Apple butter,"
 Back up he swims
  Past sting-ray and shark,
  Out with a zoom,
   A whoop, a bark;
   Before you can say
    Whatever you wish,
     He plops at your side
      With a mouthful of fish!

William Jay Smith

Giraffes

Stilted creatures,
Features fashioned as a joke,
Boned and buckled,
Finger painted,

They stand in the field
On long-pronged legs
As if thrust there.
They airily feed,
Slightly swaying,
Like hammer-headed flowers.

Bizarre they are,
Built silent and high,
Ornaments against the sky.
Ears like leaves
To hear the silken
Brushing of the clouds.

Sy Kahn

The Snakes

I once saw two snakes,
northern racers,
hurrying through the woods,
their bodies
like two black whips
lifting and dashing forward;
in perfect concert
they held their heads high
and swam forward
on their sleek bellies;
under the trees,
through vines, branches,
over stones,
through fields of flowers,
they traveled
like a matched team
like a dance
like a love affair.

Mary Oliver

Why Nobody Pets the Lion at the Zoo

The morning that the world began
The Lion growled a growl at Man.

And I suspect the Lion might
(If he'd been closer) have tried a bite.

I think that's as it ought to be
And not as it was taught to me.

I think the Lion has a right
To growl a growl and bite a bite.

And if the Lion bothered Adam,
He should have growled right back at 'im.

The way to treat a Lion right
Is growl for growl and bite for bite.

True, the Lion is better fit
For biting than for being bit.

But if you look him in the eye
You'll find the Lion's rather shy.

He really wants someone to pet him.
The trouble is: his teeth won't let him.

He has a heart of gold beneath
But the Lion just can't trust his teeth.

John Ciardi

The Bat

By day the bat is cousin to the mouse.
He likes the attic of an aging house.

His fingers make a hat about his head.
His pulse beat is so slow we think him dead.

He loops in crazy figures half the night
Among the trees that face the corner light.

But when he brushes up against a screen,
We are afraid of what our eyes have seen:

For something is amiss or out of place
When mice with wings can wear a human face.

Theodore Roethke

Deer Hunt

Because the warden is a cousin, my
mountain friends hunt in summer when the deer
cherish each rattler-ridden spring, and I
have waited hours by a pool in fear
that manhood would require I shoot or that
the steady drip of the hill would dull my ear
to a snake whispering near the log I sat
upon, and listened to the yelping cheer
of dogs and men resounding ridge to ridge.
I flinched at every lonely rifle crack,
my knuckles whitening where I gripped the edge
of age and clung, like retching, sinking back,
then gripping once again the monstrous gun—
since I, to be a man, had taken one.

Judson Jerome

Dear Danny Ledbetter

Is your face still freckled and round?
Do you smell like old pennies in a sweaty palm?
Does your unruly hair rebel in an Indian feather cowlick
As it did in the days when your father's belt
Hung on the back of his armchair, ever ready?
Do you still love doodlebugs and slip-n-slide
And are your knees skinned and scarred
From running faster than your feet can understand?
Do you skateboard at breakneck speed down the sidewalk
      on Melody Lane
      (kuthum, kuthum across the cracks)
And careen around cars on a bicycle with playing cards
      clothespinned to the spokes?
Do you sneer at the faint-hearted (bugscreaming,
      bloodsqueamish, dark-afraid)
And do you cry in deep hard pillow sobs when
      the pound truck picks up
      the stray you've been hiding?

And am I still your girl?

                    Mignon Mabry

Sembly

Sittin where Miz Pettry sets us
loudest boys, soze she can keep one
eye on us. Aint no one eye keep
Tyrones elbow outta my ribs
or pre-vent Spaz, sittin behind
fum markin my shirt—I magine
Mama yellin, How in a world
you get them ink-pen marks back here?
Ain't nothing take out ink-pen, Boy

I check the stage n theres Lurene
the girl I like. Players all wearin
black pants n skirts n shoes, white tops
an only one girl in the band—
Lurene, playin drums. They doin
"Dancin Roun Our Hemisphere" n
Lurene whomps the kettle drums n
grins. They ever make me dance at
school, I hope I get Lurene. Then
Tyrone talkin loud when Miz Bloom

nounce the final tune, I dont hear
its name, but everybody blows
loud as Spaz's Boom Box did be-
fore Miz Pettry sent that sucker
down to Lost and Found. One cold day
in Hell, she say, he bring that boom
box back. Lurene holdin cymbals
big as pans. She grins, n then POW!
That girl, she be ringin my chimes.

Stephen Dunning

34

Adolescence—I

In water-heavy nights behind grandmother's porch
We knelt in the tickling grasses and whispered:
Linda's face hung before us, pale as a pecan,
And it grew wise as she said:
    "A boy's lips are soft,
    As soft as baby's skin."
The air closed over her words.
A firefly whirred near my ear, and in the distance
I could hear streetlamps ping
Into miniature suns
Against a feathery sky.

            Rita Dove

In the Plaza We Walk

In the plaza we walk
under the Mexican moon
full of tangerine smells.

A cart pulls over
full of the fruit
full of the moon
        and the lonely star.

So we buy two
but he says "three for a peso"
        but we buy two.

Tangerines peeled
            we walk
        hand in hand
        spitting the seeds
            for future tangerines
        and more lovers to be.

In the plaza we walk
        under tangerine moons.

Nephtalí De León

A Love Song

Do I love you?
I'll tell you true.

Do chickens have lips?
Do pythons have hips?

Do penguins have arms?
Do spiders have charms?

Do oysters get colds?
Do leopards have moles?

Does a bird cage make a zoo?
Do I love you?

Raymond R. Patterson

Valentine

by Donald Hall

Chipmunks jump, and
Greensnakes slither.
Rather burst than
Not be with her.

Bluebirds fight, but
Bears are stronger.
We've got fifty
Years or longer.

Hoptoads hop, but
Hogs are fatter.
Nothing else but
Us can matter.

final note to clark

they had it wrong,
the old comics.
you are only clark kent
after all. oh,
mild mannered mister,
why did i think you could fix it?
how you must have wondered
to see me taking chances,
dancing on the edge of words,
pointing out the bad guys,
dreaming your x-ray vision
could see the beauty in me.
what did i expect? what
did i hope for? we are who we are,
two faithful readers,
not wonder woman and not superman.

Lucille Clifton

Steam Shovel

The dinosaurs are not all dead.
I saw one raise its iron head
To watch me walking down the road
Beyond our house today.
Its jaws were dripping with a load
Of earth and grass that it had cropped.
It must have heard me where I stopped,
Snorted white steam my way,
And stretched its long neck out to see,
And chewed, and grinned quite amiably.

Charles Malam

On Watching the Construction of a Skyscraper

Nothing sings from these orange trees,
Rindless steel as smooth as sapling skin,
Except a crane's brief wheeze
And all the muffled, clanking din
Of rivets nosing in like bees.

Burton Raffel

The Builders

I told them a thousand times if I told them once:
Stop fooling around, I said, with straw and sticks;
They won't hold up; you're taking an awful chance.
Brick is the stuff to build with, solid bricks.
You want to be impractical, go ahead.
But just remember, I told them; wait and see.
You're making a big mistake. Awright, I said,
But when the wolf comes, don't come running to me.

The funny thing is, they didn't. There they sat,
One in his crummy yellow shack, and one
Under his roof of twigs, and the wolf ate
Them, hair and hide. Well, what is done is done.
But I'd been willing to help them, all along,
If only they'd once admitted they were wrong.

Sara Henderson Hay

Apartment House

A filing-cabinet of human lives
Where people swarm like bees in tunneled hives,
Each to his own cell in the towered comb,
Identical and cramped—we call it home.

Gerald Raftery

The Garden Hose

In the gray evening
I see a long green serpent
With its tail in the dahlias.

It lies in loops across the grass
And drinks softly at the faucet.

I can hear it swallow.

Beatrice Janosco

How Things Work

Today it's going to cost us twenty dollars
To live. Five for a softball. Four for a book,
A handful of ones for coffee and two sweet rolls,
Bus fare, rosin for your mother's violin.
We're completing our task. The tip I left
For the waitress filters down
Like rain, wetting the new roots of a child
Perhaps, a belligerent cat that won't let go
Of a balled sock until there's chicken to eat.
As far as I can tell, daughter, it works like this:
You buy bread from a grocery, a bag of apples
From a fruit stand, and what coins
Are passed on helps others buy pencils, glue,
Tickets to a movie in which laughter
Is thrown into their faces.
If we buy a goldfish, someone tries on a hat.
If we buy crayons, someone walks home with a broom.
A tip, a small purchase here and there,
And things just keep going. I guess.

Gary Soto

Crossing Kansas by Train

The telephone poles
have been holding their
arms out
a long time now
to birds
that will not
settle there
but pass with
strange cawings
westward to
where dark trees
gather about
a waterhole. This
is Kansas. The
mountains start here
just behind
the closed eyes
of a farmer's
sons asleep
in their workclothes.

Donald Justice

Advice to Travelers

A burro once, sent by express,
His shipping ticket on his bridle,
Ate up his name and his address,
And in some warehouse, standing idle,
He waited till he like to died.
The moral hardly needs the showing:
Don't keep things locked up deep inside—
Say who you are and where you're going.

Walker Gibson

African Sunrise

Sky
Over the last star;
The parrot-winds
Sharp-beaked with yellow
Nipping the bunched date palms...

Now the camels
Open their beeswax eyes
And raise long necks,
Rutted sound in their throats—
Camels, pock-marking the sand with spread knees,
Lifting the odor of under-body with them.

Sun—
The burn of it
Hot-coined to each eyelid,
And desert-stretched,
the caravan of hours
not yet begun.

Gertrude May Lutz

Trying to Name What Doesn't Change

Roselva says the only thing that doesn't change
is train tracks. She's sure of it.
The train changes, or the weeds that grow up spidery
by the side, but not the tracks.
I've watched one for three years, she says,
and it doesn't curve, doesn't break, doesn't grow.

Peter isn't sure. He saw an abandoned track
near Sabinas, Mexico, and says a track without a train
is a changed track. The metal wasn't shiny anymore.
The wood was split and some of the ties were gone.

Every Tuesday on Morales Street
butchers crack the necks of a hundred hens.
The widow in the tilted house
spices her soup with cinnamon.
Ask her what doesn't change.

Stars explode.
The rose curls up as if there is fire in the petals.
The cat who knew me is buried under the bush.

The train whistle still wails its ancient sound
but when it goes away, shrinking back
from the walls of the brain,
it takes something different with it every time.

Naomi Shihab Nye

I Was a Skinny Tomboy Kid

I was a skinny tomboy kid
who walked down the streets
with my fists clenched into
        tight balls.
I knew all the roofs
and back yard fences,
    I liked travelling that way
      sometimes
   not touching
      the sidewalks
      for blocks and blocks
        it made
       me feel
   victorious
     somehow
over the streets.
I liked to fly
   from roof
     to roof
       the gravel
        falling
          away
beneath my feet,
       I liked
         the edge
       of almost
not making it.
  and the freedom
     of riding
    my bike
      to the ocean
and smelling it
   long before
I could see it,

and I travelled disguised
   as a boy
  (I thought)
     in an old army jacket
    carrying my
      fishing tackle
       to the piers, and
         bumming bait
       and a couple of cokes
and catching crabs
       sometimes and
     selling them
to some chinese guys
   and i'd give
    the fish away,
I didn't like fish
    I just liked to fish
    and I vowed
     to never
       grow up
    to be a woman
   and be helpless
      like my mother
but then I didn't realize
  the kind of guts
  it often took
    for her to just keep
   standing
where she was.

I grew like a thin, stubborn weed
watering myself whatever way I could
believing in my own myth
    transforming my reality
      and creating a
        legendary/self
every once in a while
    late at night
      in the deep
    darkness of my sleep
      I wake
        with a tenseness
in my arms
    and I follow
    it from my elbow to
      my wrist
and realize
    my fists are tightly clenched
and the streets come grinning
    and I forget who I'm protecting
and i coil up
    in a self/mothering fashion
      and tell myself
it's o.k.

      Alma Luz Villanueva

At Pymatuning Dam

At Pymatuning Dam
In Western Pennsylvania
The fish all have a mania
For buttered bread and jam.

A few prefer some treat,
Like tarts with fruits and jellies,
To fatten their fish bellies —
What lucky children eat.

But what do they get fed?
Loaves of week-old bread!
It keeps them so upset.
And every bit gets wet.

That's why the fish are zanier —
They want their bread and jam
In Western Pennsylvania
At Pymatuning Dam.

Raymond R. Patterson

Wonder Wander

in the afternoon the children walk like ducks
like geese
like from here to there
eyeing bird-trees puppy dogs candy windows
sun balls ice cream wagons
lady bugs rose bushes fenced yards vacant lots
tall buildings
and other things
big business men take big business walks
wear big business clothes
carry big business briefcases talk about
big business affairs in
big business voices
young girls walk pretty on the streets
stroll the avenues linger by
shop windows   wedding rings   lady hats
shiny dresses   fancy shoes
whisper like turkey hens   passing the time
young men stride on parade   dream headed
wild eyed   eating up the world
with deep glances   rubbing empty fingers
in their empty pockets and
planning
me, I wander around soft-shoed   easy-legged
watching the scene as it goes
finding things   sea-gull feathers   pink baby roses
every time I see a letter on the sidewalk
I stop and look   it might be
      for me

Lenore Kandel

Reflections Dental

How pure, how beautiful, how fine
Do teeth on television shine!
No flutist flutes, no dancer twirls,
But comes equipped with matching pearls.
Gleeful announcers all are born
With sets like rows of hybrid corn.
Clowns, critics, clergy, commentators,
Ventriloquists and roller skaters,
M.C.s who beat their palms together,
The girl who diagrams the weather,
The crooner crooning for his supper—
All flash white treasures, lower and upper.
With miles of smiles the airwaves teem,
And each an orthodontist's dream.

'Twould please my eye as gold a miser's—
One charmer with uncapped incisors.

Phyllis McGinley

The Microscope

Anton Leeuwenhoek was Dutch.
He sold pincushions, cloth, and such.
The waiting townsfolk fumed and fussed
As Anton's dry goods gathered dust.

He worked, instead of tending store,
At grinding special lenses for
A microscope. Some of the things
He looked at were:
                    mosquitoes' wings,
the hairs of sheep, the legs of lice,
the skin of people, dogs, and mice;
ox eyes, spiders' spinning gear,
fishes' scales, a little smear
of his own blood,
                  and best of all,
the unknown, busy, very small
bugs that swim and bump and hop
inside a simple water drop.

Impossible! Most Dutchmen said.
This Anton's crazy in the head.
We ought to ship him off to Spain.
He says he's seen a housefly's brain.
He says the water that we drink
Is full of bugs. He's mad, we think!

They called him dumkopf, which means dope.
That's how we got the microscope.

                           Maxine W. Kumin

Child

on Top

of a

Greenhouse

The wind billowing out the seat of my britches,
My feet crackling splinters of glass and dried putty,
The half-grown chrysanthemums staring up like accusers,
Up through the streaked glass, flashing with sunlight,
A few white clouds all rushing eastward,
A line of elms plunging and tossing like horses,
And everyone, everyone pointing up and shouting!

Theodore Roethke

**Husbands
and
Wives**

Husbands and wives
*   With children between them*
Sit in the subway;
*   So I have seen them.*

One word only
*   From station to station;*
So much talk for
*   So close a relation.*

*   Miriam Hershenson*

This Is Just to Say

I have eaten
the plums
that were in
the icebox

and which
you were probably
saving
for breakfast

Forgive me
they were delicious
so sweet
and so cold.

William Carlos Williams

Near Roscoe and Coldwater

*(the Northeast
San Fernando Valley, 1985)*

i. Sunday

*This is a busy corner.
Truckdrivers, businessmen, lowriders,
all slow down to view
the building of the Thai temple.
On the vacant lot next to gas stations
and a closed down 7-11, the roof of gold appears.
Barefoot men in orange robes
plant grass and small shade trees.
Every Sunday immigrants drive in,
they follow the light
reflected in the golden roof.
I hear chanting sounds and afterwards
the easy laughter of families
cooking lunch on outdoor grills.
They fill the neighborhood with Eastern scents,
above the car fumes and dry weed.*

ii.   Boy's Story

*He is eighteen and no matter
how many times I mispronounce his name,
he always smiles, an old man's face.
I am his only Asian teacher
since he left Kampuchea.
I've read, argued, marched
and now after seeing a film about the war,
I have the audacity to ask what he knows.
"My father killed by Khmer Rouge.
Brother killed too. Mother escaped,"
but he may never find her.
Still smiling, he tells me about
his new car. Now and then I see him,
cruising Victory Boulevard.*

Amy Uyematsu

60

Magic Story for Falling Asleep

When the last giant came out of his cave
and his bones turned into the mountain
and his clothes turned into the flowers,
nothing was left but his tooth
which my dad took home in his truck
which my granddad carved into a bed

which my mom tucks me into at night
when I dream of the last giant
when I fall asleep on the mountain.

Nancy Willard

Moon of Popping Trees

Outside the lodge,
the night air is bitter cold.
Now the Frost Giant walks
with his club in his hand.
When he strikes the trunks
of the cottonwood trees
we hear them crack
beneath the blow.
The people hide inside
when they hear that sound.

But Coyote, the wise one,
learned the giant's
magic song,
and when Coyote sang it,
the Frost Giant slept.

Now when the cottonwoods
crack with frost again
our children know, unless
they hear Coyote's song,
they must stay inside,
where the fire is bright
and buffalo robes
keep us warm.

Joseph Bruchac & Jonathan London

Nocturnal Sounds

Trembling November winds,
steam whistling in tenement pipes
breathing of slumbering neighbors
cracking walls, dripping faucets,
soft music from the flat below,
transistorized repetition of
yesterday's history.

Nocturnal sounds.

Loneliness caressing the night
and its sound is loud and penetrating.
Bursting in the eardrums like love
bursts in the heart of a new bride.

Nocturnal sounds.

Fire engines rushing to right here,
no where. Speeding cars, noisy buses,
a laughter.

Nocturnal sounds.

Sleep comes to close the ears of
the mind to night sounds of this world.

Kattie M. Cumbo

Theory of Why the Night Comes

The blue sky gets tired
The silver light of the moon
turns into a broom
And starts sweeping blue
sheets
Slowly the horizon changes
into a nightgown
And jumps over the moon
Into the mouth of the sun
Which takes it with it
To fry bamboo shoots
In China.

Victor Hernandez Cruz

Night Sight in Manlius

tail lights disappear into darkness
on the road past chuck watson's house
like red bananas
sucked swiftly back inside
a vast black peel

Keith Gilyard

At Second and Granite

Behind the playground
Garbage bags slump
Like dead bodies,
A cop car on the corner
Of the intersection
By the bridge,
Frankie & Ivan
Holding hands
With Ann & Monique
As they cross a dirt lot;
Two blocks down an old man
Turns off the television,
Stares out his third-floor
Window, stares at the sky,
At the big yellow moon;
In a corner store a kid
Makes change for two
Tall, rough looking men,
Wonders if this will
Be the night, lets out
A breath as they leave;
A young mother turns,
Squints her eyes, thinks
Of how tired she's been
Kisses her daughter
Goodnight, goodnight,
Goodnight, sweet Marie.

Sean Thomas Dougherty

**Autobiography
in Five Short Chapters**

by Portia Nelson

Chapter I
I walk down the street.
　　There is a deep hole in the sidewalk.
　I fall in.
　I am lost...I am helpless.
　　It isn't my fault.
It takes forever to find a way out.

Chapter II
I walk down the same street.
　　There is a deep hole in the sidewalk.
　I pretend I don't see it.
　I fall in again.
I can't believe I am in this same place.
　　But it isn't my fault.
It still takes a long time to get out.

Chapter III
I walk down the same street.
　　There is a deep hole in the sidewalk.
　I see it is there.
　I still fall in...it's a habit...but,
　　my eyes are open.
　　I know where I am.
It is my fault.
I get out immediately.

Chapter IV

I walk down the same street.
　　There is a deep hole in the sidewalk.
　I walk around it.

Chapter V
I walk down another street.

English as a Second Language

The underpaid young teacher
prints the letters t, r, e, e
on the blackboard and imagines
forests and gardens springing up
in the tired heads of her students.

But they see only four letters;
a vertical beam weighed down
by a crushing crossbar
and followed by a hook,
and after the hook, two squiggles,
arcane identical twins
which could be spying eyes
or ready fists, could be handles,
could be curled seedlings, could take root,
could develop leaves

Lisel Mueller

The Lesson of the Sugarcane

My mother opened her eyes wide
at the edge of the field
ready for cutting,
"Take a deep breath,"
                she whispered,
"There is nothing as sweet:
Nada más dulce."
              Overhearing,
Father left the flat he was changing
in the road-warping sun,
and grabbing my arm, broke my sprint
toward a stalk:
"Cane can choke a little girl: snakes hide
where it grows over your head."

And he led us back to the crippled car
where we sweated out our penitence,
for having craved more sweetness
than we were allowed,
more than we could handle.

              Judith Ortiz Cofer

Photograph of Managua

The man is not cute.
The man is not ugly.
The man is teaching himself
to read.
He sits in a kitchen chair
under a banana tree.
He holds the newspaper.
He tracks each word with a finger
and opens his mouth to the sound.
Next to the chair the old V-Z rifle
leans at the ready.
His wife chases a baby pig with a homemade
broom and then she chases her daughter running
behind the baby pig.
His neighbor washes up with water from the barrel
after work.
The dirt floor of his house has been swept.
The dirt around the chair where he sits
has been swept.
He has swept the dirt twice.
The dirt is clean.
The dirt is his dirt.
The man is not cute.
The man is not ugly.
The man is teaching himself
to read.

June Jordan

Born Old

Suppose we were born old.
Impossible, of course,
but suppose that we emerged
from tombs,
twig-loose bones rattling,
new breath shaking
ancient rib cages,
so that we sat or squatted
by our birth-holes,
wrinkled eyelids fluttering
mysteriously open,
or tottered out of cemeteries
squalling,
yet growing younger by the minute.

Suppose we were born wise,
filled with earth-knowing,
self-assured as lizards,
and then, grew young;
bodies turning fleshy, full and vivid,
swifter with each
immaculate moment,
shedding dry skin like people-serpents,
stepping into our years backwards,
with old age finished.

What progression
into innocence,
hair growing thicker,
skin soft as peach fuzz,
each new birthday
with one less candle on the cake,
till we approached
the games of children,
and were lost in hide and seek,
then finally, the finding of parents,
the noisy rattle in the hand,
the last "Ma-ma" and "Da-da,"
and the final
disappearance in the womb.

How differently
we'd look at children,
feeling
our memory and knowledge seeping
out of our ever-younger bones
knowing that tomorrow
we'd be eight years old, and lose
the memory of being
nine and ten.
What loves had we already forgotten
as wisdom dropped to the bottom
of infancy's transparent pool?

                    Jane Roberts

Fifteen   *South of the Bridge on Seventeenth*
I found back of the willows one summer
day a motorcycle with engine running
as it lay on its side, ticking over
slowly in the high grass. I was fifteen.

I admired all that pulsing gleam, the
shiny flanks, the demure headlights
fringed where it lay; I led it gently
to the road and stood with that
companion, ready and friendly. I was fifteen.

We could find the end of a road, meet
the sky on out Seventeenth. I thought about
hills, and patting the handle got back a
confident opinion. On the bridge we indulged
a forward feeling, a tremble. I was fifteen.

Thinking, back farther in the grass I found
the owner, just coming to, where he had flipped
over the rail. He had blood on his hand, was pale—
I helped him walk to his machine. He ran his hand
over it, called me good man, roared away.

I stood there, fifteen.

William Stafford

War

Dawn came slowly,
almost not at all.
The sun crept over the hill
cautiously
fearful of being hit
by mortar fire.

Dan Roth

Résumé

Razors pain you;
Rivers are damp;
Acids stain you;
And drugs cause cramp.
Guns aren't lawful;
Nooses give;
Gas smells awful;
You might as well live.

Dorothy Parker

Prayer

lighten up

why is Your hand
so heavy
on just poor
me?

Answer

this is the stuff
I made the heroes
out of
all the saints
and prophets and things
had to come by
this

Lucille Clifton

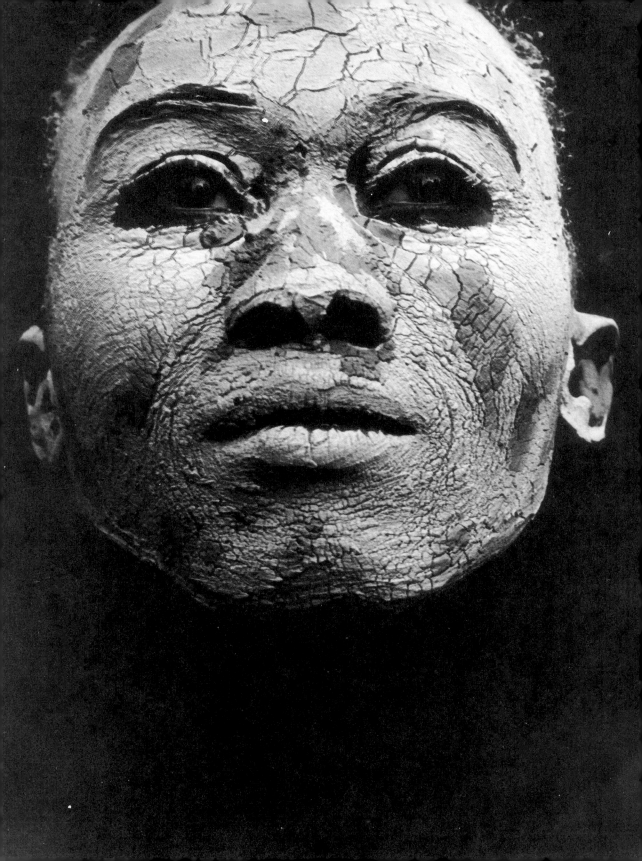

Too Blue

I got those sad old weary blues.
I don't know where to turn.
I don't know where to go.
Nobody cares about you
When you sink so low.

What shall I do?
What shall I say?
Shall I take a gun and
Put myself away?

I wonder if
One bullet would do?
Hard as my head is,
It would probably take two.

But I ain't got
Neither bullet nor gun—
And I'm too blue
To look for one.

Langston Hughes

Dust

Agatha Morley
All her life
Grumbled at dust
Like a good wife.

Dust on a table,
Dust on a chair,
Dust on a mantel
She couldn't bear.

She forgave faults
In man and child
But a dusty shelf
Would set her wild.

She bore with sin
Without protest,
But dust thoughts preyed
Upon her rest.

Agatha Morley
Is sleeping sound
Six feet under
The mouldy ground.

Six feet under
The earth she lies
With dust at her feet
And dust in her eyes.

    Sydney King Russell

Boy at the Paterson Falls

I am thinking of that boy who bragged about the day he threw
  a dog over and watched it struggle to stay upright all
  the way down.
I am thinking of that rotting carcass on the rocks,
and the child with such power he could call to a helpless
  thing as if he were its friend, capture it, and think of
  the cruelest punishment.
It must have answered some need, some silent screaming in a
  closet, a motherless call when night came crashing;
it must have satisfied, for he seemed joyful, proud, as if he
  had once made a great creation out of murder.
That body on the rocks, its sharp angles, slowly took the shape of
  what was underneath, bones pounded, until it lay on the bottom
  like a scraggly rug.
Nothing remains but memory—and the suffering of those who
  would walk into the soft hands of a killer for a crumb of bread.

Toi Derricotte

Playmate

                    And because
of him, the small box carried at shoulder
height, high school boys somber in
black and cracking no smiles missed
football practice, stood, the heavy
little box rubbing one shoulder, awkward,
bearing down

                From the church—singing.
I pulled the collar of my peajacket tight,
I sat across the street in the cold winds
preceding Spring trying to imagine Charlie:
him letting anyone keep him in that satin box.
All that crying, and him hating roses, getting
dressed up when it wasn't even Sunday, lying
there, in that sissy box.

                                Keith Wilson

We Have a Beautiful Mother

*We have a beautiful
mother
Her hills
are buffaloes
Her buffaloes
hills.*

*We have a beautiful
mother
Her oceans
are wombs
Her wombs
oceans.*

*We have a beautiful
mother
Her teeth
the white stones
at the edge
of the water
the summer
grasses
her plentiful
hair.*

*We have a beautiful
mother
Her green lap
immense
Her brown embrace
eternal
Her blue body
everything
we know.*

Alice Walker

Earth

*"A planet doesn't explode of itself," said drily
The Martian astronomer, gazing off into the air—
"That they were able to do it is proof that highly
Intelligent beings must have been living there."*

John Hall Wheelock

Southbound on the Freeway

A tourist came in from Orbitville,
parked in the air, and said:

The creatures of this star
are made of metal and glass.

Through the transparent parts
you can see their guts.

Their feet are round and roll
on diagrams or long

measuring tapes, dark
with white lines.

They have four eyes.
The two in back are red.

Sometimes you can see a five-eyed
one, with a red eye turning

on the top of his head.
He must be special—

the others respect him
and go slow

when he passes, winding
among them from behind.

They all hiss as they glide,
like inches, down the marked

tapes. Those soft shapes,
shadowy inside

the hard bodies—are they
their guts or their brains?

May Swenson

Chernobyl

At our table a world away —
the fruit, the fine tea,
the lovely meat,
the green & gold vegetables.

The world wavers
as if seen through heat
shimmering from the pavement.

The newspaper
in front of me
blurs.

Here is what we've been told to do:

1. Filter each breath four times,
   one for each direction
   the air might come from.

2. Wash all water before washing.
   (Do not drink any.)

3. Remove your skin
   before entering the house.

4. Hose down your bed
   before sleeping in it.

5. Wear your bright white suit
   to all weddings
   and funerals.

Grace Butcher

The Last Wolf

The last wolf hurried toward me
through the ruined city
and I heard his baying echoes
down the steep smashed warrens
of Montgomery Street and past
the few ruby-crowned highrises
left standing
their lighted elevators useless

Passing the flicking red and green
of traffic signals
baying his way eastward
in the mystery of his wild loping gait
closer the sounds in the deadly night
through clutter and rubble of quiet blocks
I heard his voice ascending the hill
and at last his low whine as he came
floor by empty floor to the room
where I sat
in my narrow bed looking west, waiting
I heard him snuffle at the door and
I watched

He trotted across the floor
he laid his long gray muzzle
on the spare white spread
and his eyes burned yellow
his small dotted eyebrows quivered

Yes, I said.
I know what they have done.

Mary TallMountain

Song for the Deer
and Myself to Return On

by Joy Harjo

This morning when I looked out the roof window
before dawn and a few stars were still caught
in the fragile weft of ebony night
I was overwhelmed. I sang the song Louis taught me:
a song to call the deer in Creek, when hunting,
and I am certainly hunting something as magic as deer
in this city far from the hammock of my mother's belly.
It works, of course, and deer came into this room
and wondered at finding themselves
in a house near downtown Denver.
Now the deer and I are trying to figure out a song
to get them back, to get all of us back,
because if it works I'm going with them.
And it's too early to call Louis
and nearly too late to go home.

Comforting a Grey Whale Trapped by Ice

The women lean from the jagged lip
of ice, over sudden cold water and hold
each other steady: a fist grips
the thickness of another's heavy coat.

They can barely bend, layered as they are
against the cold; their breath steams
under wreaths of parka fur, their faces
peer, old from squinting into snow.

Their hands stretch bare, and strong, and young
somehow, as they reach across the broken line
of ice and water to touch the bouldered hump
dark and rough with ice—it hardly looks

alive, vague and eyeless as it is, this strange
end of a being larger than life, this glimpse alone
larger than all the women put together, the tip
of a world vast and dark and very cold—

but the women reach out to comfort
its sad rounded curve
with the same strong hands
they use to hold each other.

Kelley Terwilliger

Wind and Glacier Voices

Laguna man said,
I only heard that glacier scraping
once, thirty thousand years ago.
My daughter was born then.

> *—a storytelling, continuing*
> *voice—*

West of Yuma, a brown man murmurs
the motion of the solar wind.

> *—a harsh, searing*
> *voice—*

Please don't tell me
how to live;
I've always lived this way.

> *—a protesting*
> *voice—*

The last time I was in Fargo
I thought I heard the echo
of a glacier scraping.

> *—a remembering,*
> *beckoning*
> *voice—*

And the wind, solar,
the big wind will come.
Solar, it will come.
It will pass by and through
and with everything.

> *—a longing, whispering,*
> *prophetic*
> *voice—*

Simon J. Ortiz

SECTION 13

Puppy   *Catch and shake the cobra garden hose.*
Scramble on panicky paws and flee
The hiss of tensing nozzle nose,
Or stalk that snobbish bee.

The back yard world is vast as park
With belly-tickle grass and stun
Of sudden sprinkler squalls that arc
Rainbows to the yap yap sun.

Robert L. Tyler

Sunning   *Old Dog lay in the summer sun*
Much too lazy to rise and run.
He flapped an ear
At a buzzing fly.
He winked a half opened
Sleepy eye.
He scratched himself
On an itching spot,
As he dozed on the porch
Where the sun was hot.
He whimpered a bit
From force of habit
While he lazily dreamed
Of chasing a rabbit.
But Old Dog happily lay in the sun
Much too lazy to rise and run.

James S. Tippett

For a Dead Kitten

Put the rubber mouse away,
Pick the spools up from the floor,
What was velvet-shod, and gay,
Will not want them any more.

What was warm, is strangely cold.
Whence dissolved the little breath?
How could this small body hold
So immense a thing as Death?

Sara Henderson Hay

Catalogue

Cats sleep fat and walk thin.
Cats, when they sleep, slump;
When they wake, stretch and begin
Over, pulling their ribs in.
Cats walk thin.

Cats wait in a lump,
Jump in a streak.
Cats, when they jump, are sleek
As a grape slipping its skin—
They have technique.
Oh, cats don't creak.
They sneak.

Cats sleep fat.
They spread out comfort underneath
    them
Like a good mat,
As if they picked the place
And then sat;
You walk around one
As if he were the city hall
After that.

If male,
A cat is apt to sing on a major scale;
This concert is for everybody, this
Is wholesale.
For a baton, he wields a tail.

(He is also found,
When happy, to resound
With an enclosed and private sound.)

A cat condenses.
He pulls in his tail to go under bridges,
And himself to go under fences.
Cats fit
In any size box or kit,
And if a large pumpkin grew under one,
He could arch over it.

When everyone else is just ready to go
    out,
The cat is just ready to come in.
He's not where he's been.
Cats sleep fat and walk thin.

Rosalie Moore

The Fisher

At half past four, mornings in June,
He met the sliding, whispery sound
Of Four Mile Brook, and liked the tune,
And liked the log road, morning-hushed;
His bare feet liked the dew-soaked ground.

At half past ten, he was headed for home,
Having tried his last last-hole for luck;
The heat and noise of the day had come,
But his bones were cool with the brookside shade,
And his ears kept the whirlpool's silvery suck.

Lyle Glazier

Hunting

Song

by Donald

Finkel

The fox came lolloping, lolloping,
Lolloping. His tongue hung out
And his ears were high.
He was like death at the end of a string
When he came to the hollow
Log. Ran in one side
And out of the other. O
He was sly.

The hounds came tumbling, tumbling,
Tumbling. Their heads were low
And their eyes were red.
The sound of their breath was louder than death
When they came to the hollow
Log. They held at one end
But a bitch found the scent. O
They were mad.

The hunter came galloping, galloping,
Galloping. All damp was his mare
From her hooves to her mane.
His coat and his mouth were redder than death
When he came to the hollow
Log. He took in the rein
And over he went. O
He was fine.

The log, he just lay there, alone in
The clearing. No fox nor hound
Nor mounted man
Saw his black round eyes in their perfect disguise
(As the ends of a hollow
Log). He watched death go through him,
Around him, and over him. O
He was wise.

The Trap

by William Beyer

"That red fox,
Back in the furthest field,
Caught in my hidden trap,
Was half mad with fear.
During the night
He must have ripped his foot
From the cold steel.
I saw him early this morning,
Dragging his hurt leg,
Bleeding a path across the gold wheat,
Whining with the pain;
His eyes like cracked marbles.
I followed as he moved,
His thin body pulled to one side
In a weird helplessness.
He hit the wire fence,
Pushing through it
Into the deep, morning corn,
And was gone."
The old man looked around the kitchen
To see if anyone was listening.
"Crazy red fox,
Will kill my chickens no longer.
Will die somewhere in hiding."
He lit the brown tobacco carefully,
Watching the blue smoke rise and disappear
In the movement of the air.
Scratching his red nose slowly,
Thinking something grave for a long moment,
He stared out of the bright window.
"He won't last long with that leg," he said.
The old man turned his head
To see if his wife was listening.
But she was deep in thought,
Her stained fingers
Pressing red berries in a pie.
He turned his white head
Toward the open window again.
"Guess I'll ride into the back field, first thing.
Some mighty big corn back there this year.
Mighty big corn."
His wife looked up from her work,
Smiled almost secretly to herself,
And finished packing the ripe berries
Into the pale crust.

Forgive My Guilt

by Robert P. Tristram Coffin

Not always sure what things called sins may be,
I am sure of one sin I have done.
It was years ago, and I was a boy,
I lay in the frostflowers with a gun,
The air ran blue as the flowers, I held my breath,
Two birds on golden legs slim as dream things
Ran like quicksilver on the golden sand,
My gun went off, they ran with broken wings
Into the sea, I ran to fetch them in,
But they swam with their heads high out to sea,
They cried like two sorrowful high flutes,
With jagged ivory bones where wings should be.

For days I heard them when I walked that headland
Crying out to their kind in the blue,
The other plovers were going over south
On silver wings leaving these broken two.
The cries went out one day; but I still hear them
Over all the sounds of sorrow in war or peace
I have ever heard, time cannot drown them,
Those slender flutes of sorrow never cease.
Two airy things forever denied the air!
I never knew how their lives at last were spilt,
But I have hoped for years all that is wild,
Airy, and beautiful will forgive my guilt.

escape

theodore R. the III
finally
got past aunt clelia uncle
dan and the
heavy glassed front
door which
protected
him from the
Other Kids
and ran ran ran ran ran ran ran
ran ran ran ran ran
ran ran ran ran
ran ran ran ran ran
it
took seven
Other Kids
to catch him:
gently —for
they greatly admired
his defiance...
aunt clelia only stood there
damp handed
on the
empty front
porch

Mari Evans

Ajo, cebolla y chile rojo

On certain summer days
breaking out in a
mopping/scrubbing/washing kinda sweat
I catch that hint of my mother
floating around

My head drops
back into her lap
where my braids were tugged into place
that hint of my mother
mixing with the ajo, cebolla y chile rojo

On certain summer days
breaking out in a certain sweat
I can't tell if it's me
or if it's her essence
that she braided into my hair.

Maria S. Limón

Combing

Bending, I bow my head
And lay my hand upon
Her hair, combing, and think
How women do this for
Each other. My daughter's hair
Curls against the comb,
Wet and fragrant—orange
Parings. Her face, downcast,
Is quiet for one so young.

I take her place. Beneath
My mother's hands I feel
The braids drawn up tight
As a piano wire and singing,
Vinegar-rinsed. Sitting
Before the oven I hear
The orange coils tick
The early hour before school.

She combed her grandmother
Mathilda's hair using
A comb made out of bone.
Mathilda rocked her oak wood
Chair, her face downcast,
Intent on tearing rags
In strips to braid a cotton
Rug from bits of orange
and brown. A simple act,

Preparing hair. Something
Women do for each other,
Plaiting the generations.

Gladys Cardiff

I Ask My Mother to Sing

She begins, and my grandmother joins her.
Mother and daughter sing like young girls.
If my father were alive, he would play
his accordion and sway like a boat.

I've never been in Peking, or the Summer Palace,
nor stood on the great Stone Boat to watch
the rain begin on Kuen Ming Lake, the picnickers
running away in the grass.

But I love to hear it sung;
how the waterlilies fill with rain until
they overturn, spilling water into water,
then rock back, and fill with more.

Both women have begun to cry.
But neither stops her song.

Li-Young Lee

Fences

Mouths full of laughter,
the turistas come to the tall hotel
with suitcases full of dollars.

Every morning my brother makes
the cool beach sand new for them.
With a wooden board he smooths
away all footprints.

I peek through the cactus fence
and watch the women rub oil
sweeter than honey into their arms and legs
while their children jump waves
or sip drinks from long straws,
coconut white, mango yellow.

Once my little sister
ran barefoot across the hot sand
for a taste.

My mother roared like the ocean,
"No. No. It's their beach.
It's their beach."

Pat Mora

My Father's Hands

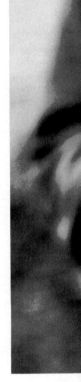

I have hands like my father,
   always in motion.
   Stirring sugared coffee
   before hoeing his rows of beans.
   He grew the best chili,
      the hottest were his pride,
      pointing to the fresh ones,
      he'd laugh and say,
      "Hot and mean like me."
He was stabbed once in a fight
   in the center of his right palm,
   damaging his fingers,
   that never fully healed.
   His middle finger slanted stiffly inward,
   though his grip remained firm.
Such steady hands my father had,
   carving
   past midnight
   into Gia's black bowls
   Drawing perfect lines
   in delicate strokes,
   a simple pocketknife his only tool.
His were the hands that lifted me,
   when I was just a girl,
   tugging playfully at my hair,
   that curled behind my ear.
   His hands,
   narrow and skilled,
   copper colored and calloused,
   weather chapped and strong.
I have hands like my father,
   I know this myself,
      but like hearing my daughter say so.

Nora Naranjo-Morse

Aunt

by Al Young

She talks too loud, her face
a blur of wrinkles & sunshine
where her hard hair shivers
from laughter like a pine tree
 stiff with oil & hotcombing

O & her anger realer than gasoline
slung into fire or lighted mohair
She's a clothes lover from way back
but her body's too big to be chic
or on cue so she wear what she want
People just gotta stand back &
take it like they do Easter Sunday when
the rainbow she travels is dry-cleaned

She laughs more than ever in spring
stomping the downtowns, Saturday past
work, looking into JC Penney's checking
out Sears & bragging about how when she
feel like it she gon lose weight &
give up smokin one of these sorry days

Her eyes are diamonds of pure dark space
& the air flying out of them as you look
close is only the essence of living
to tell, a full-length woman, an aunt
brown & red with stalking the years

Planting Shirt

by Demetrice A. Worley

*A blue cotton smock hangs in my closet. In this smock
my cousin Lois planted tomatoes and collard greens
beside her garage. Called it her planting shirt.
Told me, "When I plant my seedlings with this shirt
on, I don't lose the young ones."*

                *Once I saw her
look up from placing thin, stringy roots in the
dirt, and the faded, blue smock made the gray in
her brown eyes flutter.*

                *I told her she only wore it
to make the plants take pity on her. Now, I wear
the shirt. I remember Lois' seedlings, and I plant
my sorrow deep.*

Granny

Granny had a way with fruit trees
        Hear me now
She mixed fruit slices in her dough
        Knew just how
When she wasn't busy in her kitchen
        Baking bread
She balanced baskets with her produce
        On her head

She filled her baskets with her fruitbread
        Took her time
Put pawpaw, mango, pomegranate
        Guava and lime
She sauntered to the village market
        Easy pace
She stepped out better than a queen
        Had more grace

But she'd sass you if you vexed her, mon
        What I found
No car could move her out the road
        Stood her ground
She'd turn and shake a fist and shout,
        "Want a lickin'?
        Mash me down, nuh
        You t'ink me name chicken!"

Ashley Bryan

Pajarita

Safety in things
her hands tell her secret

small, gray Mexican bird
brittle of bone, flutters at ninety
through the large American cage
all the comforts
except youth

each day knits, knits
as her grandchildren chatter round her
sounds she'll never understand
holds tight to yarn and needle
afraid to slow and tie loose ends of life.

At night when the family gathers
round the set, she settles in her closet,
her tiny chapel, squeezes her rosary
through dry fingers, clucks litany
after litany behind the closed door
where she keeps the sherry
she sips to slip her into sleep

but all night her fingers flitter
over the cool sheets, touching
always touching
so as not to slip away.

Pat Mora

Women

They were women then
My mamma's generation
Husky of voice—Stout of
Step
With fists as well as
Hands
How they battered down
Doors
And ironed
Starched white
Shirts
How they led
Armies
Headragged Generals
Across mined
Fields
Booby-trapped
Ditches
To discover books
Desks
A place for us
How they knew what we
Must know
Without knowing a page
Of it
Themselves.

Alice Walker

Sooner or Later

sooner or later
somebody dies
in your family
& you got to know
what to do
or you are going
to feel bad
when the women
pull out
their handkerchiefs
& your hands
are still
in your pockets

  Sam Cornish

Videos

I will want to hear their voices
after they die. Those drawls
rooted like mimosa and pine
in the clay of Alabama.

I can feel their r's
heal the jags in me,
while my own tongue
searches for its
lost language.

At ninety, Aunt Lele wheezes
into the phone. "You come, now,
you heah. Sweet child,
you heah me!"

My kin are going.
The tapes are not made.
I can still catch
their humped wrinkles
swinging on the porch,
see them stiffen
shyly on camera.

The trip must be made.
Their stick fingers
shake in my face.
Come on. Come on.

Jean Arnold

SECTION 16

Foul Shot

by Edwin A. Hoey

With two 60's stuck on the scoreboard
And two seconds hanging on the clock,
The solemn boy in the center of eyes,
Squeezed by silence,
Seeks out the line with his feet,
Soothes his hands along his uniform,
Gently drums the ball against the floor,
Then measures the waiting net,
Raises the ball on his right hand,
Balances it with his left,
Calms it with fingertips,
Breathes,
Crouches,
Waits,
And then through a stretching of stillness,
Nudges it upward.

The ball
Slides up and out,
Lands,
Leans,
Wobbles,
Wavers,
Hesitates,
Exasperates,
Plays it coy
Until every face begs with unsounding screams—

And then

        And then

                And then,

Right before ROAR-UP,
Dives down and through.

The Base Stealer

by Robert Francis

Poised between going on and back, pulled
Both ways taut like a tightrope-walker,
Fingertips pointing the opposites,
Now bouncing tiptoe like a dropped ball
Or a kid skipping rope, come on, come on,
Running a scattering of steps sidewise,
How he teeters, skitters, tingles, teases,
Taunts them, hovers like an ecstatic bird,
He's only flirting, crowd him, crowd him,
Delicate, delicate, delicate, delicate—now!

Mystery

One Friday night
Mom pulled out
Learning to Dance is Fun
with diagrams of feet
and a long-play record,
while Dad watched,
like a patient
awaiting
the dentist's whining drill.

Mom counted softly
onetwo
onetwothree
through
    fox trot
        samba
            cha-cha-cha
as Dad danced—
feet on the wrong legs.

Yet,
the next afternoon
before the ball left the bat
Dad danced deep
into the hole at short,
lunged,
backhanded
in the middle of a bad hop—
the ball
at the edge of the webbing—
then
twirling,
falling away:
a perfect peg
to first.

                Paul Janeczko

The Latest Latin Dance Craze

First
You throw your head back twice
Jump out onto the floor like a
Kangaroo
Circle the floor once
Doing fast scissor works with your
Legs
Next
Dash towards the door
Walking in a double cha cha cha
Open the door and glide down
The stairs like a swan
Hit the street
Run at least ten blocks
Come back in through the same
Door
Doing a mambo-minuet
Being careful that you don't fall
And break your head on that one
You have just completed your first
Step.

Victor Hernandez Cruz

Make Music with Your Life

Make music with your life
a
 jagged
silver tune
cuts every deepday madness
into jewels   that you wear

Carry 16 bars of old blues
wit/you
everywhere you go
walk thru the azure sadness
howlin
Like a guitar player

Bob O'Meally

Piano Man

Piano Man
Will you remember the notes
Whose names you can not call
And even if you knew them
Would not dare
Call their names
For fear of displeasing
Some spirit

Your fingers skip over
The keys like children
In a game of hopscotch
The fast ones

Step on a crack
Break your mama's back

No broken backs
No missing chords
The spirits are all
Around your finger minds
They know before your
Brain does
How is that?

Joyce Carol Thomas

Wheels

by Jim Daniels

My brother kept
in a frame on the wall
pictures of every motorcycle, car, truck:
in his rusted out Impala convertible
wearing his cap and gown
waving
in his yellow Barracuda
with a girl leaning into him
waving
on his Honda 350
waving
on his Honda 750 with the boys
holding a beer
waving
in his first rig
wearing a baseball hat backwards
waving
in his Mercury Montego
getting married
waving
in his black LTD
trying to sell real estate
waving
back to driving trucks
a shiny new rig
waving
on his Harley Sportster
with his wife on the back
waving
his son in a car seat
with his own steering wheel
my brother leaning over him
in an old Ford pickup
and they are
waving
holding a wrench a rag
a hose a shammy
waving.

My brother helmetless
rides off on his Harley
waving
my brother's feet
rarely touch the ground—
waving waving
face pressed to the wind
no camera to save him.

The Sacred

After the teacher asked if anyone had
          a sacred place
and the students fidgeted and shrank

in their chairs, the most serious of them all
          said it was his car,
being in it alone, his tape deck playing

things he'd chosen, and others knew the truth
          had been spoken
and began speaking about their rooms,

their hiding places, but the car kept coming up,
          the car in motion,
music filling it, and sometimes one other person

who understood the bright altar of the dashboard
          and how far away
a car could take him from the need

to speak, or to answer, the key
          in having a key
and putting it in, and going.

                              Stephen Dunn

Seconds of Free Fall and Chaos

My bored brother dragged me
away from kiddie land, shoved me
roughly to the adult ticket booth,
the line dividing me from men.

Thrilled by tickets snaking from his fist,
I entered the kingdom of risks—
the hammer and zipper, the roller coaster,
I flinched when the hammer

slammed down, when the zipper toppled
and flipped us, I held the bar
in a car jerked up a track
and watched treetops and tents

fall away. My brother leaned close
and hissed how many fell
from these seats last year, flung out
over screaming mothers. He raised both hands

and made me, the crossbar loose on my lap.
Older boys tossed their hair
and laughed, the heads of girls
snug in their elbows.

Our car crawled on cables
grinding like bicycle chains
about to break, all rides of childhood
behind me, my arms high in surrender,

my skull wobbling
through tight turns, mashed down,
like being born again to bright lights
and dazzling screams.

Walter McDonald

April   *by Marcia Masters*

It's lemonade, it's lemonade, it's daisy.
It's a roller-skating, scissor-grinding day;
It's gingham-waisted, chocolate flavored, lazy,
With the children flower-scattered at their play.

It's the sun like watermelon,
And the sidewalks overlaid
With a glaze of yellow yellow
Like a jar of marmalade.

It's the mower gently mowing,
And the stars like startled glass,
While the mower keeps on going
Through a waterfall of grass.

Then the rich magenta evening
Like a sauce upon the walk,
And the porches softly swinging
With a hammockful of talk.

It's the hobo at the corner
With his lilac-sniffing gait,
And the shy departing thunder
Of the fast departing skate.

It's lemonade, it's lemonade, it's April!
A water sprinkler, puddle winking time,
When a boy who peddles slowly, with a smile remote and holy,
Sells you April chocolate flavored for a dime.

in Just-

in Just-
spring   when the world is mud-
luscious the little
lame balloonman

whistles   far   and wee

and eddieandbill come
running from marbles and
piracies and it's
spring

when the world is puddle-wonderful

the queer
old balloonman whistles
far   and   wee
and bettyandisbel come dancing

from hop-scotch and jump-rope and

it's
spring
and
      the

          goat-footed

balloonMan   whistles
far
and
wee

                              E. E. Cummings

Four Little Foxes

Speak gently, Spring, and make no sudden sound;
For in my windy valley, yesterday I found
New-born foxes squirming on the ground—
                Speak gently.

Walk softly, March, forbear the bitter blow;
Her feet within a trap, her blood upon the snow,
The four little foxes saw their mother go—
                Walk softly.

Go lightly, Spring, oh, give them no alarm;
When I covered them with boughs to shelter them from harm,
The thin blue foxes suckled at my arm—
                Go lightly.

Step softly, March, with your rampant hurricane;
Nuzzling one another, and whimpering with pain,
The new little foxes are shivering in the rain—
                Step softly.

Lew Sarett

Swift Things Are Beautiful   *by Elizabeth Coatsworth*

Swift things are beautiful:
Swallows and deer,
And lightning that falls
Bright-veined and clear,
Rivers and meteors,
Wind in the wheat,
The strong-withered horse,
The runner's sure feet.

And slow things are beautiful:
The closing of day,
The pause of the wave
That curves downward to spray,
The ember that crumbles,
The opening flower,
And the ox that moves on
In the quiet of power.

Counting-out Rhyme

Silver bark of beech, and sallow
Bark of yellow birch and yellow
    Twig of willow.

Stripe of green in moosewood maple,
Colour seen in leaf of apple,
    Bark of popple.

Wood of popple pale as moonbeam,
Wood of oak for yoke and barn-beam,
    Wood of hornbeam.

Silver bark of beech, and hollow
Stem of elder, tall and yellow
    Twig of willow.

Edna St. Vincent Millay

Summons

Keep me from going to sleep too soon
Or if I go to sleep too soon
Come wake me up. Come any hour
Of night. Come whistling up the road.
Stomp on the porch. Bang on the door.
Make me get out of bed and come
And let you in and light a light.
Tell me the northern lights are on
And make me look. Or tell me clouds
Are doing something to the moon
They never did before, and show me.
See that I see. Talk to me till
I'm half as wide awake as you
And start to dress wondering why
I ever went to bed at all.
Tell me the walking is superb.
Not only tell me but persuade me.
You know I'm not too hard persuaded.

Robert Francis

flowers

by Safiya Henderson-Holmes

in new york city
there are people

skin sun browned
hands earth worn

tongues as foreign
as their eyes

they push carts
filled with flowers

long stemmed, paper wrapped
and rubber banded too tightly

like the rest of the city
fragrance and color near gone

yet the people
push the flower carts

block after unyielding block
stopping to sell what they can

stopping to pray over
what they cannot

Bill Hastings

Listen to me, college boy, you can
keep your museums and poetry and string quartets
'cause there's nothing more beautiful than
line work. Clamp your jaws together
and listen:
    It's a windy night, you're freezing the teeth out
of your zipper in the ten below, working stiff
jointed and dreaming of Acapulco, the truck cab.
Can't keep your footing for the ice, and
even the geese who died to fill your vest
are sorry you answered the call-out tonight.
You drop a connector and curses
take to the air like sparrows who freeze
and fall back dead at your feet.
Finally you slam the SMD fuse home.
Bang. The whole valley lights up below you
where before was unbreathing darkness.
In one of those houses a little girl
stops shivering. Now that's beautiful,
and it's all because of you.

Todd Jailer

The Gentry

It is summer and we sit on the front porch
facing the street. We are the folks who
live in town.

Every day at three, we watch the trail
of piled trucks ascend the hill. When the road shivers,
I stand against the door. Their loads have sheared
the branches of our oaks and chunks of coal
are left behind.

I comfort the trees, stroke their barks.
I pick up a piece of coal. It is clean and shiny
and the ridges are sharp, the surface, smooth.

When the miners come home, some drive past
with their windows open and talk loudly.
The others walk by us alone. We are silent.
With white rings around their eyes, they swing
their silver buckets and call me "miss."

None of the neighbors are miners. They wear gloves
in the garden and lunch with their wives. They do not
keep watch with us. They talk among themselves.
I stand against their fence with my chunk of coal.

Elmaz Abinader

Mississippi John Hurt

mississippi john hurt
a little man
rings around his eyes
big hat
that he took off
to say hello

mississippi john hurt
plays
wearing a vest
a round black hat
a little man
mr hurt
rings under his eyes

sings
a man behind a mule
sings as he works
a little man
works as he sings
mississippi john
big eyed
mississippi john

Sam Cornish

Like an Animal

Behind the smooth texture
Of my eyes, way inside me,
A part of me has died:
I move my bloody fingernails
Across it, hard as a blackboard,
Run my fingers along it,
The chalk white scars
That say I AM SCARED,
Scared of what might become
Of me, the real me,
Behind these prison walls.

Jimmy Santiago Baca

The Forecast

Perhaps our age has driven us indoors.
We sprawl in the semi-darkness, dreaming sometimes
Of a vague world spinning in the wind.
But we have snapped our locks, pulled down our shades,
Taken all precautions. We shall not be disturbed.
If the earth shakes, it will be on a screen;
And if the prairie wind spills down our streets
And covers us with leaves, the weatherman will tell us.

Dan Jaffe

Leaves—All Over the Place—As If

by Cid Corman

Leaves—all over the place—as if
I and everyone had won
an infinite lottery or

some crazy old zillionaire had
gone and thrown away his money
before us—as if he and we

might forego these riches to sit
amidst them under the bare trees
and feel what merely being means.

Fall

by Sally Andresen

The geese flying south
In a row long and V-shaped
Pulling in winter.

This is a quiet poem.
Black people don't write
many quiet poems
because what we feel
is not a quiet hurt.
And a not-quiet hurt
does not call
for muted tones.

A Quiet Poem

by Pinkie Gordon Lane

But I will write a poem
about this evening
full of the sounds
of small animals, some fluttering
in thick leaves, a smear
of color here and there—
about the singing of crickets
and the whisper of darkness
a gray wilderness of light
descending, touching,
breathing.

I will write a quiet poem
immersed in shadows
and mauve colors
and spots of white
fading into deep tones
of blue.

This is a quiet evening
full of hushed singing
and light that has no
ends, no breaking
of the planes, or brambles
thrusting out.

**Soy Hija
de Mis Padres**

by Lorenza Calvillo-Craig

soy hija de mis padres
    nieta de mis abuelos
    hermana de mis hermanos
    prima de mis primos
    amiga de mis amigos

soy lorenza
    lencha
    lorraine
    wa
    panzas *y*
    mija
yo soy
soy
yo

**I Am the Daughter
of My Parents**

I am the daughter of my parents
    granddaughter of my grandparents
    sister of my brothers
    cousin of my cousins
    friend of my friends

I am lorenza
    lencha
    lorraine
    wa
    panzas *and*
    daughter
I am
I am
me

Saying Yes

"Are you Chinese?"
"Yes."

"American?"
"Yes."

"Really Chinese?"
"No...not quite."

"Really American?"
"Well, actually, you see..."

But I would rather say
yes

Not neither-nor,
not maybe,
but both, and not only

The homes I've had,
the ways I am

I'd rather say it
twice,
yes

Diana Chang

Invisible Indian

A few weeks ago
the cashier at the grocery store,
seeing my dark hair
and dark eyes,
counted my change
back to me in Spanish.

Three days later
the waitress at the pizza place
made the same mistake.
Happens all the time
since I moved to Miami.
As though without buckskin, braids and beads
I don't exist.

At a pow-wow last Sunday
I spoke to a Cherokee
wearing faded black jeans and a tee shirt
standing beside a display of stone sculptures.
I told him I admired his work.

He didn't mistake me for Hispanic
but saw that I was Indian
and even guessed my tribe.
Other Indians always recognize me.

Maybe they hear the echoes of the drums
in the rhythms of my voice,
glimpse the shadows of my Indian grandmother
in the chiseled cheekbones of my face,
or see the turquoise in my heart.

Deloras (Dee) Lane

address

address
occupation
age
marital status
—perdone…
> *yo me llamo pedro*

telephone
height
hobbies
previous employers
—perdone…
> *yo me llamo pedro*
> *pedro ortega*

zip code
i.d. number
classification
rank
—perdone mi padre era
> *el señor ortega*
> *(a veces don josé)*

race

Alurista

To a Little Blond Girl of Heber, Califas

that little sister of mine
was pretty, small tender
    but also very brave
    she wore cowboy boots
    a cowboy hat t-shirt and levis
she was always followed
    by little Wienie dogs
the Chapo the Chapa and the Chapitos
once she tried to take a molar from one
with a large pair of mechanics' pliers
and during Holy Mass
when communion was offered
to be precise
she said to Father Jean Vincent
—Cabrón. I am going to tell my papa
that you didn't want to give me the
white cookie. Now
    well she's a mother   wife
       and she behaves herself.

Margarita Cota-Cardenas

How a Girl Got Her Chinese Name

On the first day of school the teacher asked me:
What do your parents call you at home?

I answered: Nellie.

Nellie? Nellie?
The teacher stressed the l's, whinnying like a horse.
No such name in Chinese for a name like Nellie.
We shall call you Nah Lei
which means Where *or* Which Place.

The teacher brushed my new name,
black on beige paper.
I practiced writing Nah Lei
holding the brush straight, dipping
the ink over and over.

After school I ran home.
Papa, Mama, the teacher says my name is Nah Lei.
I did not look my parents in the eye.

Nah Lei? Where? Which Place?
No, that will not do, my parents answered.
We shall give you a Chinese name,
we shall call you Lai Oy.

So back to school I ran,
announcing to my teacher and friends
that my name was no longer Nah Lei,
not Where, *not* Which Place,
but Lai Oy, Beautiful Love,
my own Chinese name.
I giggled as I thought:
Lai Oy *could also mean* lost pocket
depending on the heart
of a conversation.

But now in Chinese school
I was Lai Oy, *to pull out of my pocket*
every day, after American school,
even Saturday mornings,
from Nellie, from Where, *from* Which Place
to Lai Oy, *to* Beautiful Love.

Between these names
I never knew I would ever get lost.

Nellie Wong

What Happened to You?

The moment he sees me, he comes running into the peaceful
      suburban street,
hands up, palms out, a little sternly as if he's stopping
      traffic.
He trots along beside my chair. "What happened to you?"
      he asks,
serious six-year-old eyes fixed on my legs. He really wants
      to know.

Most children want to ask. Even the little ones, rolling by
      in their strollers,
look at me with round eyes, as if they wonder how I get to
      have wheels, too.
I look back at them, trying to see what looks so different.
      How they know.
Sometimes they ask if it hurts. Once a small boy asked me,
      "Are you going to die?"

I hardly ever mind, or I try not to mind. It's important
      to be matter-of-fact
and calm. I want them to know this is part of the story.
      But this afternoon,
with the quiet leaves sifting all around, when he asks his
      important question
I want to cry and scream and break down in the street:
      I don't know. I don't know.

Karen Fiser

A Short Note

to My Very Critical

and Well-Beloved

Friends and Comrades

First they said I was too light
Then they said I was too dark
Then they said I was too different
Then they said I was too much the same
Then they said I was too young
Then they said I was too old
Then they said I was too interracial
Then they said I was too much a nationalist
Then they said I was too silly
Then they said I was too angry
Then they said I was too idealistic
Then they said I was too confusing altogether:
Make up your mind! They said. Are you militant
or sweet? Are you vegetarian or meat? Are you straight
or are you gay?

And I said, Hey! It's not about my mind.

June Jordan

Some Light to Hold in My Hands

At night the trees catch stars in their branches
and hold them
the way children hold fireflies in their hands.
When I want to catch some light
and hold it in my hands
I light a candle.
I hold my fingertips up to warm them
and watch the flame breathe and tremble
like a living thing.

I am burning up as I live
but it often seems not fast enough.
I'm never bright enough
or hot enough.
I'm only melting slowly,
feeling my life drip away,
feeling my blood turn to wax in my veins,
and my head on fire;
knowing I will burn down
and soften and melt away.
The light in my body
will snuff itself out.

Instead of slow candle
I would be a quick stick of dynamite
to destroy,
or a newborn star,
a sun to warm centuries of planets,
or a firefly in the night.

I am neither brief delightful firefly
nor forever-seeming star.
The stars that collect in my branches
will fade as soon as tomorrow.
The light that I catch in my hands
will fly out through my fingers.

Harryette Mullen

Where Is The Black Community?

Where is the Black community?
Holding down the corner where
Third Street meets B and

Sitting in the second pew
At Double Rock Baptist Church

Where is the Black community?
At Bob's Barber Shop
Busting jokes about the man

And at the Delta sisters
Fashioning J. Magnin and new hairdos

Where is the Black community?
Scrubbing chitlin grease
Off a kitchen stove eye

and hawking Muhammed Speaks
on a Stanford campus

Where is the Black community?
Transplanting kidneys
In a university hospital

And plowing cotton
In a Mississippi dawn

Where is the Black community?
Teaching English at Duke
And Purdue

And arranging four kids
In a twin sized bed

Where is the Black community?
Living in two story houses
On Poplar Drive

And swilling Old Crow
Out of a crystal flask

Joyce Carol Thomas

Oregon Winter

The rain begins. This is no summer rain,
Dropping the blotches of wet on the dusty road:
This rain is slow, without thunder or hurry:
There is plenty of time—there will be months of rain.
    Lost in the hills, the old gray farmhouses
Hump their backs against it, and smoke from their chimneys
Struggles through weighted air. The sky is sodden with water,
It sags against the hills, and the wild geese,
Wedge-flying, brush the heaviest cloud with their wings.
    The farmers move unhurried. The wood is in,
The hay has long been in, the barn lofts piled
Up to the high windows, dripping yellow straws.
There will be plenty of time now, time that will smell of fires,
And drying leather, and catalogues, and apple cores.
    The farmers clean their boots, and whittle, and drowse.

Jeanne McGahey

The Stump

Today they cut down the oak.
Strong men climbed with ropes
in the brittle tree.
The exhaust of a gasoline saw
was blue in the branches.

It is February. The oak has been dead a year.
I remember the great sails of its branches
rolling out greenly, a hundred and twenty feet up,
and acorns thick on the lawn.
Nine cities of squirrels lived in that tree.
Today they run over the snow
squeaking their lamentation.

Yet I was happy that it was coming down.
"Let it come down!" I kept saying to myself
with a joy that was strange to me.
Though the oak was the shade of old summers,
I loved the guttural saw.

Donald Hall

A Snowy Mountain Song   *I like her like that,*

a white scarf
tied to her head,
and lines on her face
are strong.

Look, the snowy mountain.

Simon J. Ortiz

Dreams

Hold fast to dreams
For if dreams die
Life is a broken-winged bird
That cannot fly.

Hold fast to dreams
For when dreams go
Life is a barren field
Frozen with snow.

Langston Hughes

Leathery, wry, and rough,
Jaw full of chaw, and slits
For eyes—this guy is tough.
He climbs the slatted fence,
Pulls himself atop and sits;
Tilts back his cowboy hat,
Stained with sweat below
The crown, and wipes a dirty
Sleeve across his brow;
Then pulls the hat down tight,
Caresses up its sides,
And spits into the dust
A benediction.

Gracelessly, his Brahma bull
Lunges into the chute
And swings a baleful
Eye around, irresolute.

Rodeo   *by Edward Lueders*

Vision narrower still,
The man regards the beast.
There's weight enough to kill,
Bone and muscle fit at least
To jar a man apart.
The cowboy sniffs and hitches at
His pants. Himself all heart
And gristle, he watches as
The hands outside the chute
Prepare the sacrificial act.
Standing now, and nerving up,
He takes his final measure
Of the creature's awful back.

Then he moves. Swerving up
And into place, he pricks
The Brahma's bullish pride.

The gate swings free, and
Screams begin to sanctify
Their pitching, tortured ride.

Reflections on a Gift

of Watermelon Pickle

Received from a Friend

Called Felicity

During that summer
When unicorns were still possible;
When the purpose of knees
Was to be skinned;
When shiny horse chestnuts
   (Hollowed out
    Fitted with straws
    Crammed with tobacco
    Stolen from butts
    In family ashtrays)
Were puffed in green lizard silence
While straddling thick branches
Far above and away
From the softening effects
Of civilization;

During that summer—
Which may never have been at all;
But which has become more real
Than the one that was—
Watermelons ruled.

Thick pink imperial slices
Melting frigidly on sun-parched tongues
Dribbling from chins;
Leaving the best part,
The black bullet seeds,
To be spit out in rapid fire
Against the wall
Against the wind
Against each other;

And when the ammunition was spent,
There was always another bite:
It was a summer of limitless bites,
Of hungers quickly felt
And quickly forgotten
With the next careless gorging.

The bites are fewer now.
Each one is savored lingeringly,
Swallowed reluctantly.

But in a jar put up by Felicity,
The summer which maybe never was
Has been captured and preserved.
And when we unscrew the lid
And slice off a piece
And let it linger on our tongue:
Unicorns become possible again.

John Tobias

PHOTOGRAPH CREDITS

AUTHOR-TITLE INDEX

179